To
_____

From
_____

Date
_____

# You Can Do Tea

Written and Illustrated by

## Sandy Lynam Clough

**HARVEST HOUSE PUBLISHERS**

EUGENE, OREGON

# You Can Do Tea

Copyright © 2010 by Harvest House Publishers
Published by Harvest House Publishers
Eugene, Oregon 97402
www.harvesthousepublishers.com

ISBN 978-0-7369-2684-3

Text by Sandy Lynam Clough

Design and production by Garborg Design Works, Savage, Minnesota

**Printed in China**

10 11 12 13 14 15 16 17 18 / I M / 10 9 8 7 6 5 4 3 2 1

To

*Abigail Catherine Clough*

*and*

*Sarah Elizabeth Clough,*

*who do tea delightfully*

  # Contents

# There's Just Something About Tea

*Y*ou can do tea!
You can *do* tea!
You can do *tea*!

No matter how you say it, tea is your ticket to terrific friendship times.

*When you're pressed for time, you can do tea.*
*When you want to create a splendid event, you*
*    can do tea.*
*When your budget is tight, you can do tea.*
*When the sky is the limit, you can do tea.*
*In a cottage-sized home, you can do tea.*
*Outside on the lawn, you can do tea.*
*Even if you can't cook, you can do tea.*

Tea is the most flexible way to share hospitality that you can imagine. Not only can you do tea, but you'll find out what tea can do for you.

*Tea can connect you with a friend on the spur
of the moment.*
*Tea can adjust to any budget.*
*Tea can fit friendship into the tightest schedule.*
*Tea can express your creativity.*
*Tea can satisfy your need for beauty.*
*Tea can celebrate any occasion.*
*Tea can make you and your guests feel special.*
*Tea can fit you!*

Why *entertain* (which rhymes with "pain" and "strain") when you can do tea (which rhymes with "hospitality") and open up your heart and home, sharing what you have. And the most important thing you have to share is your love for people. Hospitality is not a mysterious talent, it is simply this: making people feel that you are genuinely glad they came—so glad that it makes them happy to be there.

My mother demonstrated hospitality to me. Teaching while she went, she shared with me the importance of manners, attractive tables, wonderful food, appropriate dress and, most of all, a welcoming spirit. She would often preface her instructions with "The book says…" Since she had studied home economics in college, I just assumed that somewhere there must be a book that was a complete authority. By the time I was an adult, I suspected that "the book" might not actually exist. "The book" is simply everything that she knew and had learned. Though I never did see "the book," I still have what was in it to use in sharing hospitality.

This is my version of "the book." I invite you to let it be your go-to and how-to for offering friendship with a cup of tea.

# CHAPTER 1

# Developing Your Own Tea Theme

There's just something about tea that makes it special—no matter how little or how much you accessorize it.

Come for tea: Come for connection. Come for joy. Come for comfort. Tea creates the atmosphere where we can simply focus on people.

Knowing that the focus of your gathering is your guest creates a "no-pressure" opportunity for you. There are unlimited choices you can make as you design your tea to your taste, your budget, your schedule, and your imagination. You can have fun going "over the top" or be elegantly simple.

It is enough to set a nice table with dishes you use every day. Actually, some of your guests may feel more comfortable if you don't fuss or go to extra effort. But the opportunity that you may find irresistible is to use your creativity to make your guests feel extra special by delighting them with a beautifully decorated table or a theme that infuses your own teatime experience with the enchantment of imaginative details.

A tea is your chance to express your

personality with your favorite motifs and collections that are "so you." Or, just for fun, you can try something new and completely different. If you tend to be elegantly tailored, just this once, you might want to try a little "froufrou." If your style is vintage or traditional, contemporary could feel very fresh. Whether you choose a tea theme with splendor or whimsy, the process of fashioning a theme can satisfy your ever-present desire to be creative. The process itself should be a joyful one for you.

Impressing your guests should not be a concern. Letting them experience the joy is all that matters.

There are countless themes to choose from—you will never run out of ideas!

## I have a theme…how do I develop it?

Let's walk through a party layer by layer, considering each element that is a possibility for carrying your theme. You can pick or choose how many you want to use.

A "Garden Tea" theme will illustrate how each element could be used.

1. Your invitation represents you first and intrigues your guest. Attaching your invitation to a little treat or symbolic memento makes it unforgettable.

   *A printed card attached to the back of a packet of flower seeds and slipped into an envelope plants seeds of expectation for a unique party.*

2. The flavors of your menu can echo your theme, as can the appearance and

presentation of the food. Sandwiches, cookies, and scones can all be cut into special shapes that repeat your theme.

*Not only can you use flower shapes at a garden tea, many tea blends include flowers, and you can use some flowers as garnishes if they have been grown completely without chemicals or pesticides and are edible, not toxic, flowers.*

*A tea "flower" that blooms where everyone can see in a glass teapot is a lovely bit of theater for the table.*

3. "Come see what's inside!" A brightly colored flag catches the eye when the house comes in view. An entrancing entrance sets the tone and will draw your guests inside. Decorate your door with a welcome wreath and add some large-scale accessories to your porch or stoop.

*A cheerful floral wreath, a wheelbarrow with pots of garden flowers, or a romantic wicker chair with a garden hat can all say "Welcome to my garden tea."*

4. Beyond the front door, the powder room will be a destination for some of your guests. Just

## Special Tea Moments

Teas are a special time for me. My daughter Tammy started having a Mother's Day Tea for myself, my 83-year-old mother, and herself about eight years ago and has had one for us every year since. On one occasion, she had us write touching things we could remember about our mothers (hers included) and read them aloud. Needless to say, we were all in (happy) tears and each of us conveyed words of love to the other that might not have been said otherwise. It was such a special time and the memories that we are making will last a lifetime.

*Ginger Engler*
*Waukomis, Oklahoma*

chandelier-style light fixture over the table? If so, hanging elements of your theme from the lights above crowns your tea table. Anything hung should be light in weight, and keep anything flammable away from warm bulbs. Christmas ornaments or even teacups can be hung with filament.

*Large paper butterflies hung with filament add movement and whimsy to a garden theme.*

6. Furniture pieces, such as a buffet, create a stage to expand your tablescape with items that won't fit on or don't belong on your table.

*You could arrange birdhouses, a bird's nest, or ceramic or painted iron birds. Stacked clay flowerpots, bulbs, and garden tools could also be added.*

a hint of your theme in your hand towels, bouquet, or a small decorative accent shows your attention to detail.

*A small watering can full of flowers says again, "Welcome to my garden."*

5. Look around at the room where you will have your tea. This is where you will create the atmosphere of your theme. Is there a

7. Cover your back! The back of a chair begs to be embellished with hanging ornaments or a big, perky bow.

*For a garden tea, a straw hat hung by a colorful ribbon says you've just come in from the garden.*

8. Your table is the very center of your party! Start with a "cover-up." A pretty tablecloth

# Ideas for Decorating

I decorate my table days ahead so I can focus on preparing food the day of the party. I want to enjoy the party as a guest too, so the more I can do ahead of time, the more relaxed I am.

I love collecting dishes, but I find that I use my solid white dinner plates the most. I have also started collecting table linens in all colors. The same white dishes look completely different on a different tablecloth. I also like to layer table linens. A pretty tablecloth with a complementary placemat, and maybe even a charger, makes a very interesting table.

A theme helps me plan the centerpiece. For a "Tea at Tiffany's" theme I've used a white box filled with Tiffany-blue tissue paper and a silver teapot tipped over, with a string of pearls pouring out of the spout in the center of the box. I scattered my collection of brooches and loose rhinestones around the base of the box.

For a travel theme, I used trunk-shaped baskets, old gloves, a passport, a map, and old brochures and postcards. For a "Kentucky Derby" tea, I used horseshoes, mint julep cups, and bright-colored silk napkins with some red roses. At a "Tea by the Sea" party I filled three glass vases with sand, layered seashells in them, and filled them with water tinted aqua with food coloring.

*Shannon Gough*
*Owensboro, Kentucky*

is the foundation of a beautiful table and "softens" it. A wide variety of tablecloths can be purchased. Pretty sheets are also an option—or you can make your own tablecloth. Spraying your tablecloth in advance with a good fabric protector (one that is appropriate for your fabric) is a good defense against stains.

Layering tablecloths is an attractive option that allows you to mix colors, textures, or prints. You can't go wrong with your mix if all the patterns share one dominant color.

*Exuberant floral tablecloths accented with fresh gingham frame a garden tea with a "just-picked" attitude.*

9. Whether you prefer pottery or china, your plates and teacups can make or break your theme. A solid color lets the food take the

spotlight, but since your plates are first seen empty, any pattern should relate to your theme. Mixing and matching can add the sparkle of variety as long as every design has color or theme in common.

*A collection of different floral plates, cups, and saucers can be reminiscent of the profusion of flowers in a cottage garden.*

10. The containers for your flowers can echo your theme, or can be clear glass and almost invisible.

*A group of three watering cans with flowers would be a perfect accent for a garden tea.*

11. Napkin holders are the "jewelry" of a tea, and they can actually be vintage jewelry pieces that you collect at flea markets. Jeweled and rhinestone pins add a touch of bling!

*"Bug," butterfly, or flower pins add a little sparkle as napkin accessories. Or, napkins can be tucked into a new, cheerful garden glove.*

12. Party favors are little mementos of your teatime and a special touch. Favors are entirely optional, not an obligation. Your

napkin accessories can do double duty and become take-home favors.

*A little blooming bedding plant is the perfect garden-tea treat!*

13. Flickering candles add the perfect glow to a lovely tea table, but save the candles with any kind of fragrance for other rooms. Candles with food, spice, or floral fragrance will compete with the aromas of your food and tea.

Now that you've reviewed a smorgasbord of options, you can pick and choose how you will present *your* theme.

# Themes for Tea

Fall, Summer, Spring, or Winter

Holiday (Christmas, Easter, Valentine's Day)

Travel

Your city or state

Flower (roses, daisies, hydrangeas, or other)

Movie (*Breakfast at Tiffany's*, *Wizard of Oz*)

Tea by the Sea

Snow and Ice

Rainy Day

Monochromatic (pick one color and use all shades)

Kentucky Derby

Picnic

Swap Tea (bring tea accoutrements and exchange them)

Princess or Queen for a Day

Paris, London, or New York

Safari

Back to School

Have You Seen My Purse?

Candlelight

Hats

Treasure Box or Jewelry Box

Polka Dot

Country French

New Beginnings

Tea Time (use clock collection)

Scrapbook Tea (old cameras for centerpiece)

Retro

Hollywood Glamour

*I Love Lucy*

Bugs (butterflies, dragonflies, and ladybugs)

Faith, Family, and Friends

A favorite hymn, song, or Scripture verse

Birds

Death by Chocolate

Cinderella

Japanese

Victorian

Mother's Day

*Shannon Gough*
*Owensboro, Kentucky*

# CHAPTER 2

# A "No-Fail, One-Size-Fits-All, Tailored-for-You" Menu

Everyone would want to have tea every day if they just knew about the food! Besides being delicious, the food is one of the tools you can use to build friendship. Conversation and connecting flow naturally around food. The food at your tea table will actually hold the group together for a period of time so that hearts can laugh, talk, and share. But creating a menu doesn't have to be a challenge. I've done it for you!

These recipes have interchangeable parts so that you can serve the "same thing" over and over, and it will still be different. You can customize them with ingredients you have on hand or with your own personal taste.

For a perfectly scrumptious tea,

*This is the only chicken salad recipe you need.*
*This is the only scone recipe you need.*
*This is the only cookie recipe you need.*
*This is the only sandwich recipe you need.*
*Add two pots of tea: one tea and one herbal (no caffeine).*
*Offer Sandy's Tea Society Crème for scones.*
*Finish with Sandy's Tea Society Cake.*

Choose and stir in 1 cup of each of the following three groups and 2 teaspoons from the herb list:

**Binder**
sour cream
mayonnaise
plain yogurt
Dijonnaise

**Sweet**
dried cranberries
raisins
dried cherries
currants
well-drained
    pineapple
chopped apple
seedless grapes

**Crunch**
chopped celery
chopped water chestnuts
chopped cabbage
chopped pecans

**Herbs/seasoning**
dried thyme
dried basil
dried oregano
garlic powder
celery seed
curry

### *Chicken Salad Your Way or "What Can I Put in Chicken Salad?"*

*Start with the basic chicken salad recipe:*
    4 cups of chopped rotisserie or baked chicken
    ½ cup of chopped onion or
        scallions (optional)
    1 teaspoon salt
    1 teaspoon pepper

*Patti Brussat*
*Roswell, Georgia*

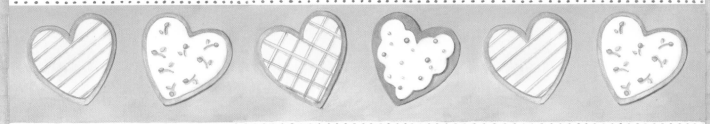

## The "What Would I Like in My Cookies?" Recipe

*Basic cookie recipe:*

Mix together with a mixer:
1 cup butter at room temperature
¾ cup of packed dark brown sugar
¾ cup of granulated sugar

Add and mix in:
2 teaspoons of vanilla or almond extract
1 teaspoon of baking soda
1 teaspoon of baking powder
2 large eggs

Stir in 3½ cups of flour (white or wheat)

*Create your own cookies:*
Fold in 2-4 cups of any of the following ingredients. You can mix and match to equal 2-4 cups of add-ins.

chopped walnuts
chopped pecans
slivered almonds
chopped macadamia nuts

peanuts
raisins
coconut
dried cranberries
chopped dates
chopped dried cherries
chocolate chips
white chocolate chips
butterscotch chips
English toffee chips
oatmeal (not instant)

To bake: Drop with a spoon on the cookie sheet, leaving 2 inches between cookies. Bake for exactly 8 minutes at 350 degrees. Allow to cool on cookie sheet for 5 minutes and then place on cookie rack to cool completely.

This dough can also be used to make bars rather than cookies. Simply spread into a 9 x 13 baking pan (I put my hands into a baggie to help spread the dough so it won't stick to my hands). When making bars, bake at 350 degrees for exactly 25 minutes.

*Patti Brussat*
*Roswell, Georgia*

## Monica's Cream Scones

Preheat oven to 425 degrees.

*Ingredients:*
2 cups all purpose flour
½ teaspoon salt
1 tablespoon baking powder
¼ cup sugar
1¼ cups heavy whipping cream
3 tablespoons melted butter
Additional sugar for sprinkling on top

Plain scones are delicious on their own, but here are some flavor options to try. Add ½ cup total of any one item below, or pick two and add ¼ cup of each. If you would like to add fresh lemon, lime, or orange zest to the dough, use 1 tablespoon of zest and mix it well into the dry ingredients before adding the cream. (You may

also add vanilla or almond extract by adding 1 teaspoon to the heavy cream before adding to the dry ingredients.)

chopped dried apricots
white chocolate chips
chocolate chips (try with orange zest)
cinnamon chips
dried cranberries (try with lemon or
    orange zest)
toffee bits
diced apple
fresh or dried blueberries (try with
    lemon zest)
diced dried pineapple
dried cherries
diced peaches (use dried if you can
    find them)
chopped almonds, macadamia nuts, pecans,
    or walnuts
coconut

*Directions:*
Combine the flour, salt, baking powder, sugar, and optional dried fruit, nuts, or zest in a medium-size mixing bowl. Pour in the heavy cream.

Using a large spoon, stir ingredients together until just combined. Turn dough out onto a floured board and knead gently 7 to 8 times just until it holds together—do not overwork dough. Gently form dough into a 7-inch round about 1 inch thick and cut into 6 or 8 wedges, or cut into the desired shape(s) using a cookie cutter. Place the scones 2 inches apart on an ungreased or parchment-lined baking sheet, or on a baking stone. Brush the tops of the scones with melted butter and sprinkle with sugar.

Bake at 425 degrees for 10-12 minutes until lightly golden brown. All ovens vary a little, so watch the bottom of the scones and don't let them get more than a light golden color. Remove from pan immediately and cool on wire rack. Store in an airtight container. Serve warm with whipped cream, lemon curd, or raspberry jam.

*Storing and reheating:*
Baked scones can be stored in an airtight container or frozen. If freezing, wrap individual scones tightly in plastic wrap and then in a resealable bag—remove as much air as possible. When needed, remove scones from plastic wrap and defrost completely, then wrap loosely in foil and reheat in 300-degree oven for 10-15 minutes.

To freeze unbaked scone dough, form scones into preferred shape and place on parchment paper-lined baking sheet. Do not brush with melted butter and sugar before freezing. Place baking sheet in the freezer until scones are frozen solid, then wrap individual scones tightly in plastic wrap and then in a resealable bag, removing as much air as possible. Return to the freezer. When needed, remove scones from plastic wrap and allow to completely defrost on parchment-lined baking sheet. Brush the tops with melted butter, sprinkle with sugar, and bake at 425 degrees for 10-12 minutes.

*Monica Duelley*
*Littlestown, Pennsylvania*

Open-faced sandwiches are always pretty with a garnish on top.

### *Sandy's Friendship Tea Sandwiches*

8 ounces cream cheese
⅔ cup crushed pineapple (well-drained, with liquid squeezed out)
¼ cup pecans, finely chopped
½ cup chopped dried apricots
butter
optional: 10 ounces of thin-sliced smoked deli ham
1 loaf of bread (white, whole-wheat, or multigrain), sliced

Mix cream cheese, pineapple, apricots, and pecans together. Spread butter on bread. Spread on cream cheese mixture. Top with a bread slice and trim crusts or cut into shapes with a cookie cutter.

### *"What Can I Add to Cream Cheese?" Sandwiches*

Cream cheese and bread are a versatile combination for party sandwiches. Do remember to spread butter on the bread before adding any filling. Also "seal" the underneath of the bread on top of the filling with butter. This helps prevent soggy sandwiches. If you are using a filling, make your sandwiches first, then trim off the crusts and cut into rectangles, diamond shapes, or finger sandwiches. If you are making an open-faced (no top) sandwich, cut your bread first.

## Sandy's Strawberry Sandwiches

8 ounces cream cheese
½ cup strawberry jam (sweetened with
  fruit juice only)
butter
fresh strawberries
1 loaf of bread (white, whole-wheat,
  or multigrain), sliced

Use mixer to mix cream cheese and strawberry jam. After spreading butter on bread, spread mixture on trimmed bread (or bread cut into shapes). Heart-shaped bread is especially pretty for these sandwiches. Top with a slice of a fresh strawberry, washed and without stem. Slicing the strawberry vertically (through the top) creates a "heart-shaped" slice.

## Cucumber Sandwiches

8 ounces cream cheese
⅔ packet of ranch salad-dressing mix
2 tablespoons of mayonnaise
1 cucumber (English cucumber if you
  can find it), peeled and sliced
butter
1 loaf of bread (white, whole-wheat,
  or multigrain), sliced

Blend salad dressing mix, cream cheese, and mayonnaise. Spread bread with butter. Spread on trimmed or cut-out bread. Top with thin cucumber slice. *Important:* 30 minutes to an hour before assembling, spread cucumber slices on a folded paper towel. Sprinkle with salt. This allows the water to drain from the slices.

### Sandy's Tea Society Cake

2 cups sugar
2 cups flour
1 teaspoon baking soda
2 teaspoons cinnamon
1 teaspoon instant coffee granules
2 sticks margarine
4 teaspoons cocoa
1 cup water
½ cup buttermilk
2 eggs
1 teaspoon vanilla
1 teaspoon orange extract

Sift together flour, sugar, baking soda, cinnamon, and coffee. Set aside. In a saucepan, melt margarine. Add cocoa and water and bring to a boil. Pour over flour mixture. Quickly add buttermilk, eggs, vanilla, and orange extract.

Mix well. Pour into a greased and floured 9 x 13 baking pan or dish. Bake at 400 degrees for 20 minutes or until top springs back when touched. Leave cake in pan.

*Icing:*
1 stick margarine, melted
4 tablespoons cocoa
6 tablespoons buttermilk
1 tablespoon vanilla
1 teaspoon instant coffee granules
1 teaspoon orange extract
1 box (3¾ cups) powdered sugar
1 cup chopped pecans or slivered almonds

In a large saucepan, combine margarine, cocoa, and buttermilk. Bring to a boil. Stir in vanilla, coffee, and orange extract. Reduce heat. Add powdered sugar and nuts. Mix well. Pour over cake. Serve when cooled.

## How to brew a pot of tea

1. To brew a proper pot of tea, begin with a stovetop kettle and a teapot.

2. Fill the kettle with cold tap water and put it on the stove, then fill the teapot with very warm tap water. The warm water "tempers" the pot so that when you pour the boiling water into it, the temperature change won't crack your beautiful china teapot. Pour this water out before you put your tea in.

3. When the water is about to boil, drop 1 teaspoon of loose tea per person into the pot and add one extra spoonful for the pot. You can use an infuser to avoid straining the tea when you pour it. If you prefer teabags, use one per person and one for the teapot.

4. Let the water come to boil in the kettle, but don't let it boil more than three or four minutes before you pour it over the tea.

5. You don't have to let the tea steep for long—three to five minutes should be sufficient. If you have used an infuser or teabags, remove them in the kitchen before serving with the teapot. If you have used loose tea, use a pretty strainer over the teacup as you pour.

# A Cup of Tea and Friendship

My daughter had spent the day shopping with a friend, and when the young lady and her mother and aunt dropped my daughter off, I asked whether the mother and her sister would like to come in for a cup of tea. They eagerly said "yes," and in the time it took the water to boil we had a tea party.

I put assorted tea bags on the table, three different cups, a glass coaster filled with sugar cubes, paper napkins, and a juice glass filled with milk. All I had were six fancy tea cookies (about the size of your finger) to offer, but they were pretty, and the ladies seem to enjoy a little taste of chocolate to nibble. One of them said, "How nice—an instant tea party." We  sat and talked for about 45 minutes while the children played in my daughter's room, and then they were on their way.

Don't hesitate to offer a cup of tea and friendship. Even if it's sudden and mismatched, your guests will have a lovely time.

*Shannon Gough*
*Owensboro, Kentucky*

28

# CHAPTER 3

# Easy Tea Etiquette

If the "E-word" has caused you hesitation about having a tea, let's demystify etiquette and learn how easy it is to do.

Yes, there is a correct way for sending an invitation, for setting a table, for serving, for eating…actually, for doing everything. But I believe that at the core of every "correctness" is the motivation to treat everyone with kindness and respect. If you put the comfort, feelings, and ease of others first, your behavior will always be correct, even if you miss a bit of protocol. The kindness is in your heart, and you won't forget it—nor will your guests.

The most comforting aspect of etiquette is that it gives you the confidence that you are serving your guests correctly. There is comfort in tradition and manners. When everyone knows what to expect and what to do next, a gathering flows beautifully. Manners create a more relaxing atmosphere, not a "stiff" one.

Let's start by reviewing the most important things you need to do and need to know. We'll consider the time-honored "standards" and some solutions for the "stickies." (The "stickies" happen when someone doesn't behave with manners or consideration.)

something unusual—like an autumn leaf for a Harvest Tea.

Your invitation should include all the elements of a good news story: who, what, when, where, and how.

*Who:* You are giving the party.
*What:* It is a tea party.
*When:* List the month, day, and year (the day of the week can be helpful); the time the party begins; and the time the party ends.
*Where:* The location. Be sure to list your full address.
*How:* Explain the dress code and the theme, if you have one. You might say *dressy, Sunday dress, casual (a broad category), holiday attire, girly-girl, or an era, such as the 1950s or the 1970s.* You may add, *hats, please,* or *gloves, please.* You may prefer to keep the party theme a surprise, but your guests will appreciate knowing how to dress appropriately.

Traditionally, written invitations include "RSVP," which is French: "Répondez s'il vous plaît," meaning "Please respond." Invited guests should respond quickly whether they are able to attend or not.

Sadly, in today's culture, in spite of the love of all things French, "RSVP" on an invitation

## Begin with the beginning— the invitation

The invitation sets the tone for all that follows. One question you may ask: to "*E*-vite" or "*in*vite"? Although E-vites work well for some occasions, a written, mailed invitation is still the gold standard for a tea. *Effort* is equated with *special.* And a mailed invitation says "special occasion" and "for a special guest."

Handwritten invitations, purchased invitations, or invitations printed from your computer are all options for you. Or you may be very creative and write your invitation on

is frequently ignored—leaving the hostess guessing. Anxious hostesses who must plan for food are either phoning those invited, trying to get a definite answer, or resigning themselves to providing for a guest that they, in their hearts, don't think will come. Yet they feel they must be prepared, "just in case."

I suggest that you consider replacing "RSVP" with a kindly worded request that suggests you will expect or prepare for the guest if you hear from her: *I am so hoping to hear that I can expect you. Please call me (phone number) or e-mail me (e-mail address) before (date).* For a large event, you might use, *My space is limited—please call if you would like me to reserve a place for you.*

This is probably the stickiest "sticky" that today's hostess faces—finding out who is actually coming. If you don't hear back from your invitation, do call and make sure the invitation arrived. This is also a good way to not only find out if the guest is coming, but also to let her know what to wear and how much you're looking forward to seeing her.

You're committed! The invitations are out and responses are coming in.

## What to wear?

If you're the hostess, in regard to what everyone will wear, you get to decide—or close to it. Choosing a dress code for the invitation is important because I think everyone does have a sense that a tea is not a "T-shirt and jeans and chip and dip" affair…but they may not have a tea dress either.

Traditional dress for a tea is a nice dress, actually—a tea dress. Take your cue from the personal style of all your guests and what you want to see at your tea. Here are some options to choose from:

1. *Sunday dress*—dressier than what you would wear to work
2. *Skirts and dresses*—which just means "no pants"
3. *Dressy casual*—pants, yes, but no T-shirts or sweats
4. *Casual*—can be interpreted as jeans and shorts
5. *Glam*—which allows fun dress up and sparkles (good for evening)
6. *Your favorite outfit you never get to wear*—this can be a conversation starter
7. *Whatever makes you feel most like a girl!*
8. *Seasonal*—such as favorite Christmas sweaters
9. *Fun accessories*—such as a "crazy hat"
10. *Costumes*—should require only minimal effort and no expense (such as "retro" or "70s"). Any more than that can discourage a guest from coming.

Any dress code you choose should be in line with what your friends actually own and wear. The idea of a dress code is to make everyone comfortable, so that the focus is on the friendship time.

## How shall we set the table?

Setting a pretty table is so much fun! Start with putting the plate for your guest in the middle of the place you are setting for her. Or *plates*—if you wish to stack a charger, a dinner plate, or dessert plate, and your menu needs them.

To the left go all forks, placed in the order they will be used starting from the outside. To the left of the forks, the napkin is placed. You may choose to place the napkin on top of the plate if you have made it especially pretty.

Now let's go to the other side. Knives go next to the plate, and spoons to the right. If there are multiples, they also are placed from the outside in, in the order they will be used. The teacup and saucer are placed above the plate and to the right.

Since this isn't a dinner party, you need to provide only the utensils you will actually use at a tea party. If all your treats are all finger food, you still will need a knife for spreading toppings on scones and a spoon for the tea. A fork is always helpful if any food falls apart or becomes "stray." A dessert fork or spoon is placed at the top of the plate.

The food itself may be served on pretty plates and platters, a three-tiered server, or both. The three-tiered server is traditional for tea and saves room on the table. One tier is for dessert treats, one for party sandwiches, and one for scones. If you don't have one, a friend may have one to loan.

Think through your menu and be sure to provide a serving utensil for every plate, tray, or bowl. Be sure to remember spoons for the clotted cream, lemon curd, or jam.

Plan ahead to keep all pets out of sight and happy during your party.

Now that you're all set, what will you do when the guests arrive?

## Follow me, girls!

You are the leader, and the guests will take their cues from you, especially if they are not sure what to do and how to do it. As you lead them through your party, you will also be gently teaching.

The party begins at the door. Station yourself there to welcome your guests. It's helpful to have a friend show each arriving guest the way to the party area so you're not drawn away from the

door. Twenty minutes past the appointed time should give ample time for all who are reasonably on time to arrive.

Lead your guests to the room where you have prepared the party. Where the hostess goes, the party goes. They're there to visit with you! So, to keep your guests from gathering (and staying) in the kitchen, have all your food preparations done before they arrive. It's good to have a friend help with the last-minute tasks of brewing tea and putting out hot scones.

## The joy of serving

If you plan to say grace, do so before you all sit down or before the food is served or passed. After you are seated, place your napkin in your lap. Food should be passed to the right, and you, as hostess, will pour the tea. You may also ask a friend to assist you and to "pour."

Some etiquette rules are just basic sanitation. Don't let any serving utensils touch your personal utensils or food. When serving yourself clotted cream or lemon curd, use the serving spoon to put a dollop on your plate, and then use your own knife to spread any on your scone. Never use the serving utensil on your scone. For the same reason, don't touch your tea or your teacup with the sugar tongs.

Swish the tea in your teacup as silently as possible. Lift the cup to sip it, but not the saucer with it. The spoon you use to "swish" can be placed on your saucer at the back of the teacup.

Take small bites of the food and enjoy the conversation. If necessary, guide the conversation to include everyone.

Replenish the food as necessary, and keep serving utensils and used silverware off the tablecloth to avoid stains.

If something doesn't go quite as you planned, remember that your plans are just a framework for providing friendship time. Forgiveness and flexibility will cover most "stickies" and increase your own enjoyment.

When you are finished and others seem to be too, place your napkin, loosely folded, on the left side of your plate. Until the tea is finished, a napkin in use may be on the lap, or on the chair if you have to get up, but not on the table.

If your stated time is up, you'll want to say a warm goodbye to each guest at the door and thank them for coming.

## Unsticking the hostess "stickies"

"Stickies" are the "Oh my!" things that people do without consideration. We could call them the "rudies," but that might not be polite. The solutions here are offered as possibilities to help you deal with the unexpected with grace, while trying to salvage your party. So what can you do if…

*…Your guest brings an extra, uninvited guest?*

It's a good idea to always plan for one or two extra. Look at it as an opportunity to make a new friend. Quickly add another place, or always have an extra place set. If there's no room at your set table, you can make a place for yourself and the new guest at a

# The Favorite Guest… And How to Be One

A gracious guest knows how to follow the leader, because it's the leader's party! She enjoys herself while, at all times, flowing with the hostess. Here are some follow-the-leader reminders:

Arrive on time. Not early, and not more than a very few minutes late.

Bring a small hostess gift: Flowers, chocolates, or maybe a nice candle.

Admire her home and decorations.

Offer help. If it's declined, don't help. If you are given a task, do only that task unless the hostess gives you another one.

Go to the table when the hostess asks.

Admire, enjoy, and appreciate what she has prepared.

Eat when the hostess begins. (Do not start eating before her.)

Contribute pleasant conversation and take an interest in everyone.

Leave no stains. Be diligent to protect the hostess's fabric napkin from your lipstick print and her tablecloth from any spilled tea or stray food.

Stop eating when she stops.

Offer thanks as you leave on time.

Send a written note of thanks the next day.

smaller table nearby where you can sit with her and make her feel welcome. Whether she feels awkward or welcome depends on you.

*…Your guest brings a child to a "ladies only" event?*

This is an opportunity to teach hospitality. Remember that the child was brought there and can't help the situation. Having a small cup and saucer on hand and accommodating a child can make an indelible impression of graciousness. How many of us relate our memories of grace and hospitality to older women we remember?

*…A guest breaks up the party by getting up and beginning to stack your dishes?*

This one is tough to stop once it is underway. It is best handled with an ounce of prevention. When your party begins, make an announcement to your guests that you know they will want to help you, but that you want to treat them today and serve them. It's important to you that they relax and visit today and let you do the clean up afterward.

*…A guest is very late?*

Feel free to go ahead and begin the party. It wouldn't be kind to have the other guests wait or to have the food past its peak. The late guest can be warmly welcomed and included when she arrives.

*…You call about an RSVP and the guest wants to be a "part-time" guest, saying she can come "an hour late" or could come and leave "an hour early"?*

This would be so disruptive to your party that it is best for you to gently discourage the part-time guest and let her know that schedule won't be possible. You might say, "I'm so sorry this date isn't workable for you. I wouldn't want you to be rushed or stressed. Let's forget this party,

and I'll send an earlier invitation
for the next one before your schedule fills up."

*…You didn't know a guest was a vegetarian?*

It's always a good idea to have at least one
non-meat sandwich in your menu and one
non-dairy sandwich to accommodate possible
diet restrictions.

*…You invite twelve and only two show up?*

Forget your disappointment quickly
and appreciate this opportunity to focus your
attention on just one or two guests. This kind
of party can end up being the best—plus there
will be more desserts all around!

*…Some of your friends just won't respond
to your offer of a tea party or just don't
show up?*

Friends have different personal styles of
connecting. Those who are uncomfortable with
invitations, responding, and definite teatimes may
be your "meet me for coffee" friends, rather than
your tea-party friends.

# CHAPTER 4

# Teatime Can Be Flexible: Fun Alternatives

## To potluck—or not to potluck

When you offer hospitality by inviting guests to your home for a gathering or party that you are giving, it is understood that you, as the hostess, are responsible for providing the food. It isn't polite to invite a guest to a tea party and expect her to share hostess duties by bringing her own food. However, you may consider asking a friend to share the work, fun, and expense of a tea as a co-hostess if lack of budget or time limits your ability to host the party by yourself.

Adjusting your menu and tea to fit your budget and time is always an option too, because tea is so flexible! Instead of giving a full tea, it is perfectly fine to invite friends for tea and scones. The goal, after all, is to gather for friendship. This kind of tea is best scheduled for mid-morning or mid-afternoon so there is no expectation of a complete meal.

Potluck parties do work well when you are opening your home and participating in a tea party that is a function of a regular group.

Whether it is a tea group, a book club, a neighborhood group, or a Sunday School class, every member should be willing to share in the expense and preparation of the food so one person doesn't bear all the cost and grow weary with the effort.

When a tea is held as a special event for a large group, potluck can work very well.

## A progressive tea

Here is another possibility if you're overwhelmed by the thought of the expense and labor of a full afternoon tea in your home. A "Progressive Afternoon Tea" might be the perfect answer. It's as easy as one, two, three.

## Wonderful Memories

A few years ago, my mother and my mother-in-law became residents of a nursing home. I saw what it meant to them for someone—me—to come from the "outside" with special teacups, plates, napkins, and tea treats and sit down for a visit, learning about them, over a cup of tea.

It was at my friend's mother's memorial service that I became aware of how much the tea parties mean to the residents and their families.

Next to the display of my friend's parents' wedding photos and other family photos was a table devoted to the monthly teas that I hosted and her mother had attended…with themes such as Teddy Bear Tea, Beach Party Tea, Mother's Day Tea, First Ladies' Tea…even a Golf Tea!

*Marylou Dunsford*
*Indialantic, Florida*

*Step one:* Invite three other ladies to join you as hostesses in their homes. If there will be eight ladies attending, you could work in pairs and still use just four homes.

Step two: Choose a date and time for your tea. Decide which lady will be responsible for sending the invitations and whether or not small favors will be provided. These costs can be shared equally. Everyone starts at the first home together and travels to each house. Allow approximately 45 minutes to an hour in each home and additional travel time between houses. When her home is next, a hostess can leave a little early to arrive at home before the guests. Or she can do the last-minute prep after everyone gets there.

*Step three:* Since an afternoon tea usually includes three courses (scones with jam and cream, savories, and sweets, in that order), decide which lady would prefer to serve each course. For a fourth, you might add a first-course soup (chilled for a summer tea, hot for a winter tea). Tea is also served with each course. Food options for quick prep and serving include entrées that can be served cold (such as chicken salad sandwiches), a casserole that has already been cooked and can be microwaved, and scones that are already baked.

*Pat Borysiewicz*
*Ocoee, Florida*

## Tea for Little Ladies

Here's another wonderful teatime alternative that shows how flexible tea can be! From dressing in pretty clothes to serving others graciously, tea parties help girls truly enjoy being girls. A tea party is the perfect way for mothers, grandmothers, and aunts to enjoy special times with their girls while giving them the lifelong advantage of learning to be ladies. A lady is always admired because she possesses all of the best qualities of womanhood and femininity.

We can describe a girls' tea party by spelling L-A-D-Y!

*L is for lots of fun.* When friends gather around a tea table, there is always lots of fun!

*A is for* always *being kind and friendly.* Teatime is a great time to treat your friends to something special and show them how much you like them.

*D is for doing the right thing.* It's easy to practice our manners and show our consideration for others at a tea party.

*Y is for yummy food.* What better way is there to learn how to prepare food that is pretty and yummy than a tea party!

Three years old is not too young to start tea parties with a well-behaved child. A child-sized table and chairs are best when little ones serve and eat—even if you have to sit on a footstool to join them.

Choose a pretty little washable tablecloth. A ceramic

or china tea set is best to teach a child how to carefully use pretty, yet breakable, things. You will find that a little girl delights in pouring the tea herself! If it overflows, just blot it up. She is learning and will soon be able to control the flow of the tea. Sharing is also reinforced as treats are passed and shared. Sugar cubes are more fun than granulated sugar because a child may not have seen them before.

Helping make the food for the tea party makes a little girl (or boy) feel very special and is part of the tea experience. A tea with just one type of cookie and one kind of sandwich is adequate...or even just a cupcake. Here are some sample menu items:

1. *Cupcakes with sprinkles.* Bake the cupcakes ahead of time. Mix a buttercream icing and let the children frost the cupcakes and add sprinkles.

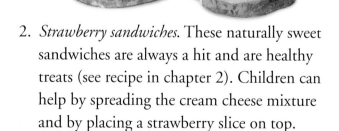

2. *Strawberry sandwiches.* These naturally sweet sandwiches are always a hit and are healthy treats (see recipe in chapter 2). Children can help by spreading the cream cheese mixture and by placing a strawberry slice on top.
3. *Tea-party-hat cookies.* Purchase two kinds of plain cookies—one smaller than the other. Vanilla wafers or mini vanilla wafers work well as the smaller cookie (which will be the "crown" of the hat). A butter cookie or other round, plain cookie should be large enough to be the "brim" of the hat when they are stacked together.

Using color icing in a tube, squeeze a dollop in the center of the larger cookie, then place the smaller one on top. This should hold them together. Then pipe a ring of icing around the edge of the smaller cookie and make a bow. You may use a different color and make little flowers all around and really get creative. These are adorable cookies that look wonderful on the cookie plate.

Children can also assemble these cookies. The girls will enjoy it tremendously, even if their "bows" are not perfect.
4. *Tea for little ones.* A fruit or herbal "tea" is best, since tea for children should not have caffeine. Raspberry might be a favorite, or peppermint.

You can easily make a tea-party play dress for your favorite little girl to wear at her make-believe—or real—little tea parties.

1. Purchase a plain T-shirt in her favorite color.

2. Purchase a pretty fabric for a skirt that coordinates with the T-shirt. Measure the length from her waist to the floor and buy twice that. For instance, if the length from her waist to the floor is ¾ of a yard, then buy 1½ yards of the fabric. You will need two ¾-yard lengths. Sew the sides together (right sides together), turn, and gather the top of the skirt. Then sew the skirt onto the bottom of the T-shirt.

3. Purchase a 2-yard length of tulle in white or a coordinating color. Put it around the waist and tie a big bow in the back. The bow is what gives the dress the "princess" feel.

This is a versatile little play dress that can be pulled over the child's head to get off and on. You can dress it up as much as you like…replacing the sleeves in the T-shirt with ruffled sleeves, or adding appliqués or sparkles to the top.

# How to Start and Maintain a Regular Tea Group

A good place to start a regular tea group is with five or six ladies who are interested in tea or are eager to learn about the custom of having tea parties. Invite them to your home for the initial tea. Even if you can find only two other ladies, don't let that hold you back. The importance of having a tea society is showing kindness and developing friendships, not trying to outdo one another with a beautiful home or fancy china.

Decide among yourselves how you would like to proceed. Home tea parties on a regular schedule with each lady taking a turn? Home tea parties on a "hit and miss" basis when the spirit moves you to invite ladies over for tea? Occasionally visiting nearby tearooms? Themed teas? When it is your turn, do you want to provide all the food, or do you want ladies to bring a dish? Either way can work.

When I started the Orlando chapter of Sandy's Tea Society in 1998, I invited two ladies to my home for tea. Those two ladies each had a tea, inviting another one of their friends, and within a few months we were up to eight members.

We run a very "loose" tea group, and it has served us well. There is never any pressure to host a tea. The ladies who love to entertain do so more frequently. Others may host only occasionally, but help out in other ways.

We have an understanding that when you are the hostess you may just invite the eight core members or you may invite one or two special friends. Occasionally members have had much larger teas with guest speakers, musicians, authors, and so on. But then the next member might bring everything back down to "reality" and just have us in for a dessert tea.

We've only had two rules: 1) no talking about medicine and medical problems, and 2) no gossip. The one tradition we have always enjoyed is wearing hats to our teas.

*Pat Borysiewicz*
*Ocoee, Florida*